If Money Could Shout

Can you imagine what I'd tell you?

By Paul Nourigat

Illustrated by eight talented artists

FarBeyond Publishing LLC

WHAT IF ....

.......Ben Franklin could describe his experiences on this particular $100 bill, after being printed on it over 40 years ago?

.......How many wallets was he in?

.......How many hands was he passed to?

.......Where in the world was he?

.......What was purchased using this bill?

.......How many times did the owners of the bill wish they had the bill back instead of spending it?

.......What warnings or encouragements would Ben SHOUT to us?

By understanding THE BRUTAL TRUTHS, teens can significantly improve their chances for financial success.

If Money Could Shout .... The Brutal Truths for Teens
FarBeyond Publishing LLC

505030109999961

Credits

Illustrators

The author selected eight illustrators from 140 applicants across America to illustrate his anthology. Each of the eight artists illustrated one of the stories in this book without visibility of the other seven artists or stories. The result is a wide range of creative genius and visual power. See artists' profiles at the end of each story.

Executive Editor, Lisa Nourigat

Steadfast support, strong perspectives and thoughtful opinions.

Book Layout, Irene Sprang

Outstanding graphical, visual and collaborative skills.

Proofing & Pre-edit, Neil Nourigat & Lauren Swett

17 year olds, seeing what the author could not.

Text and Illustrations Copyright © 2012 FarBeyond Publishing LLC

Manufactured in USA
FarBeyond Publishing LLC

If Money Could Shout .... The Brutal Truths for Teens

Library of Congress Control Number: 2012939180

Table of Contents

People are so simple of mind, and so much dominated by their immediate needs, that a deceitful person will always find plenty who are ready to be deceived.

Niccolò Machiavelli

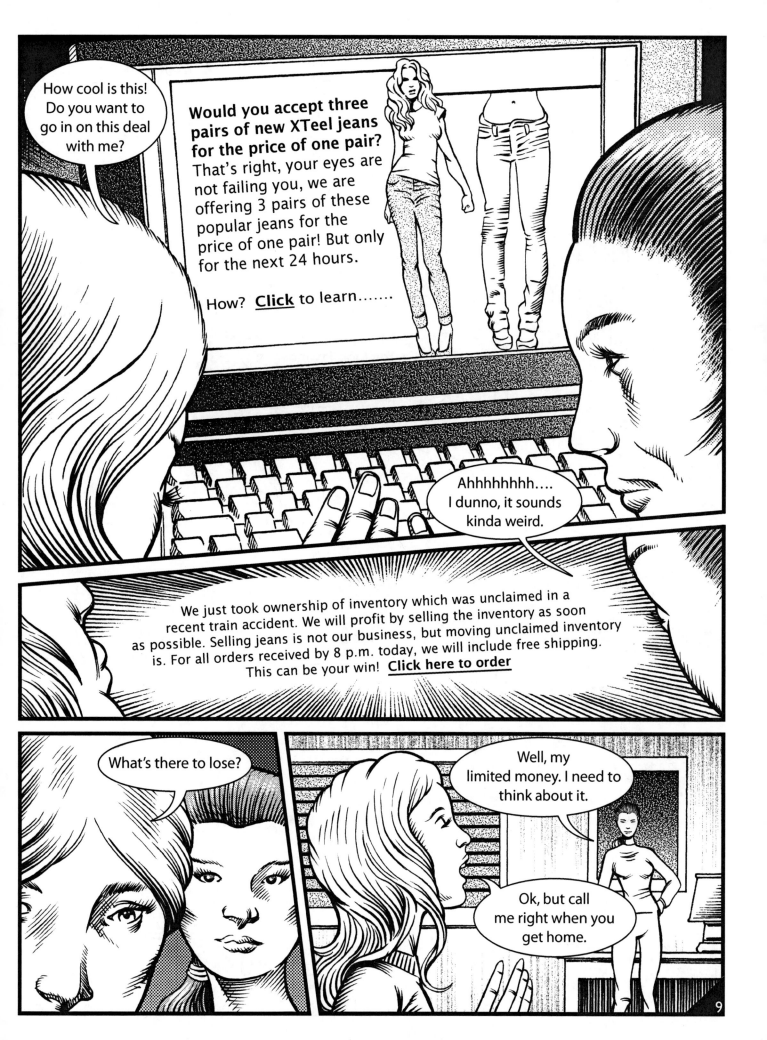

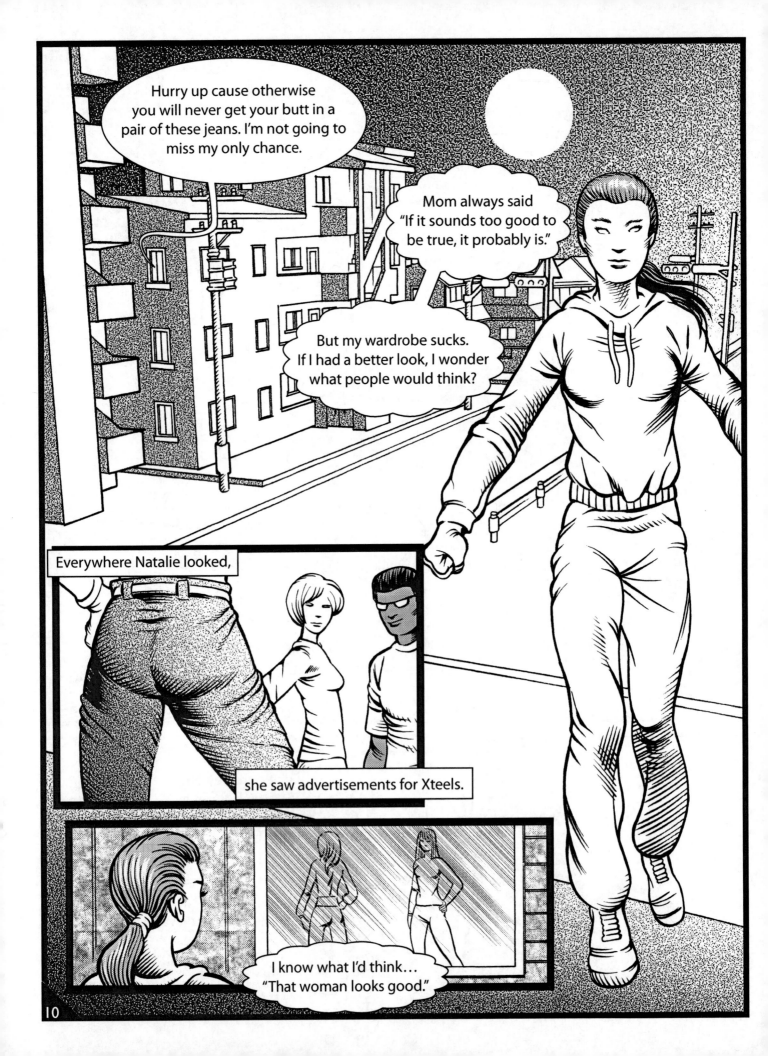

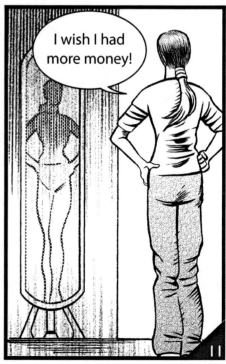

14

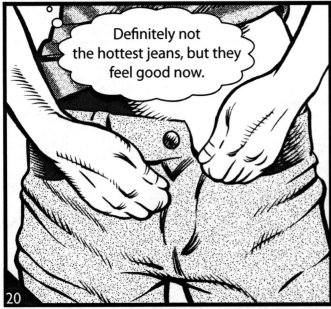

20

From the author

"A sucker is born every minute" is the modern expression for people who are taken advantage of.

The fact is, on-line scams of our time have replaced equally complex scams of the past, as thieves constantly seek what others have and conjure up new schemes to get it. This has occurred from the beginning of time.

Avoid sharing information about the specifics of your money, the places you store your money, or the financial affairs of others. It is "bad form" and a great risk.

Paul

If Money Could Shout ... the brutal truths for teens:

Illustrator Profile:
James Keefer

Not long ago, I got excited about buying vintage comic books in an online auction website, something I hadn't done in awhile so I was out of practice. I jumped in and began bidding on books to read for enjoyment and inspiration. Unfortunately I was not as cautious as I should have been. Many of the books I bought were in lesser condition than I'd hoped. I got a few great deals, but also wasted a lot of money. My lesson was to pay close attention to what I'm buying and make sure it's really what it seems to be, as is depicted in "Too Good".

Why Graphic Novels?
I am drawn to sequential art and visual storytelling. It's like making a movie, only not nearly as expensive! I grew up looking at great comic book art and have never grown tired of it.

About James......
James was born in New Orleans, LA. He loved art as a young child and began formal studies in college. After a few years of art classes at City College of San Francisco, James began a professional career by working for comic book companies. In the years that followed James did book covers, T-shirt design, concept art, graphic novel stories, oil paintings and many other assignments. Currently James lives and works in Southfield, Michigan with his wife Laurel and their dog Shawnee.

LOOKIN' FINE

It is greed to do all the talking
but not to want to listen at all.

Democritus

LOOKIN' FINE

By Paul Nourigat
Illustrated by Mark Smith

31

35

From the author

"Showing" wealth is often a sign of little wealth, or a demonstration of a personal insecurity. Acting like you have a bunch of money ultimately alienates you from many good people.

Playing that game puts a huge burden on people to keep up the pace, which can be a never-ending "stretch" for acceptance and reinforcement of their ego. Avoid it, by focusing on the things that really matter in life. Your finances will prosper as you buy the things you need, rather than what you think others think you need.

Paul

If Money Could Shout ... the brutal truths for teens:

LOOKIN' FINE

Illustrator Profile:
Mark Smith

In the story I illustrated, "Lookin' Fine," I found that I could relate to the story on a personal level. I grew up poor and it was tough seeing the other kids take for granted things I could never afford. On the other hand (and I'm embarrassed to admit this), my wife and I recently bought a new couch because we were having our neighbors over for the first time. We were planning to get a couch anyway, but I felt the pressure to "keep up with the Jones", or in our case, the Beckmans ☺

Why Graphic Novels?
I love art and I love stories and it's a no-brainer that comic books are perfect for me. What I love about graphic novels is that unlike monthly serialized comics, they offer complete stories in one place, like a movie or book.

About Mark......
Mark was born in St. Louis, MO, bounced around growing up, and found a home in Omaha, NE. Along the way he served our country in the Marine Corps, earned a degree in Electronic Imaging & Media Arts, got married, bought a house, and had a daughter. He fills his time watching his daughter during the day and pursuing a comic book career by night.

Someday

Optimism is the faith that leads
to achievement.

Nothing can be done without
hope and confidence.

Helen Keller

Dad and Mom said they felt lucky, so they spent money at casinos.

But I know where luck got our family.

They had really cool parties with their friends.

I liked it because I could eat chips and nuts after they all went to sleep.

I had to have everything cleaned up before they woke up.

43

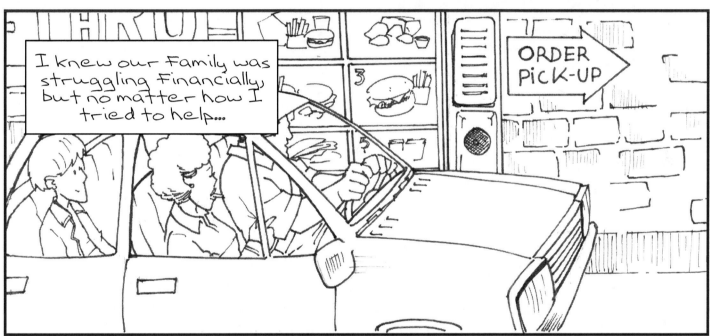

I knew our family was struggling financially, but no matter how I tried to help...

Well Mikey, someday you can do things differently.

47

49

51

From the author

No, the printer didn't mess up. If reading this upside down feels a little weird and unsettling to you, remember that's the way many people around you feel about life.

When young people are in-between things and in a tough spot in life, everything feels upside down. If you are one of those people, don't despair. You are important and will find a better place; sometimes it finds you. If you are more fortunate, be thankful - and above all be kind to those whose pain you can't imagine.

Paul

If Money Could Shout ... the brutal truths for teens:

Someday

Illustrator Profile:
Anders Eriksen

Luckily I grew up having parents who were smart with their money, so I never personally had to go through Michael's painful experiences in "Someday". But the story resembles what my wife had to go through, growing up as a child, so I can relate to the story in many ways.

Why Graphic Novels?
I feel that graphic novels offer a perfect blend of art and writing. They are an absolute free form of art, which is a natural springboard from my work in comics.

About Anders......
Anders spends most of his creative time doing special effects and story boards for films. In his art, he works primarily in pencils and grey tones. Anders is originally from Denmark, but currently lives in Philadelphia with his wife Asia, along with their dog and 5 cats. Anders travelled to the U.S. to attend trade shows and conventions and then worked on Asia's book and fell in love with her. Anders and Asia were married the following year and reside in the United States.

PAST THE HORIZON

*I run on the road, long before
I dance under the lights.*

Muhammad Ali

PAST THE HORIZON

By Paul Nourigat   Illustrated by James Beihl

58

59

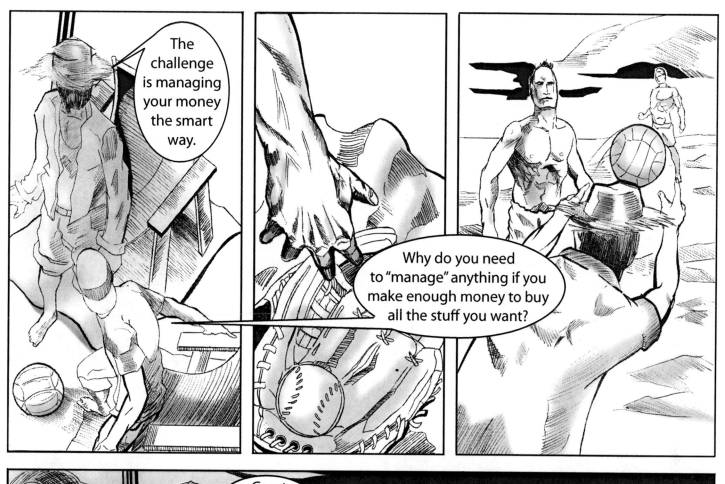

61

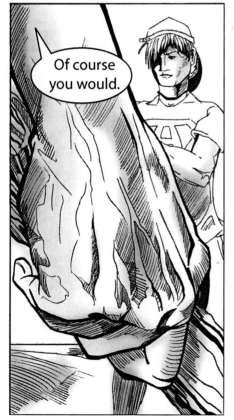

What about your car? That must have cost you a ton of money.

Yeah, but I didn't buy that cool car until much later in life, after I had saved a ton of coin.

Remember the buddies I told you about that are still struggling with money? A lot of them borrowed money so they could own cool cars right after graduation.

65

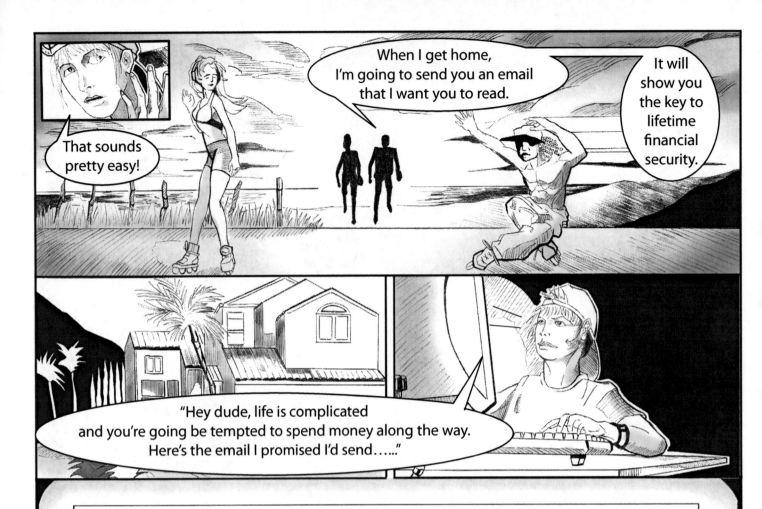

............When I was younger, I saw this formula and it changed my life.

This shows two people ("Early Saver" and "Late Saver") who made different choices. This assumes they save the same amount each year, earning 7% each year on their savings, but one chooses to save while young, and the other decides to start later. Check it out.......

Years the Investor Saved	Early Saver		Late Saver	
	Annual Savings	Total Saved	Annual Savings	Total Saved
Years 1 - 10	$ 5,000	$ 50,000	None	
Years 11-35	None		$ 5,000	$ 125,000
Interest income		$ 351,000		$ 213,000
Final balance		$ 401,000		$ 338,000

So, as you can see, people who save money early in life ("Early Saver") can rest easier for the rest of their life, because their money is growing for 25 more years. The people who spend early in life end up grinding it out for the rest of their life ("Late Saver") and still don't end up with as much as early savers. They start too late.

So, you've got to ask yourself, WHO DO YOU WANT TO BE?   Love, Gramps

From the author

It's incredibly hard to avoid the temptations to spend money. Between our wants and the endless promotions thrown at us, we're constantly conflicted on saving for the future.

A mentor taught me early in life to "pay yourself first", meaning save your money and put it away (savings, investments, etc.) before you start paying others (spending). I listened, it worked.

Paul

If Money Could Shout ... the brutal truths for teens:

PAST THE HORIZON

Illustrator Profile:
James Beihl

I agree with the key message of "Past the Horizon" to "save for the future and don't spend frivolously". I think of my great aunt; by saving for life, she was able to amass a significant amount of money. She bought a second home at age 80, with plenty of money left for her continued retirement. She's an inspiration to me.

Why Graphic Novels?
I like Graphic novels because they, like individual comic books, are examples of sequential storytelling integrating words and pictures. I feel this type of storytelling is very rich, and cinematic. It allows the reader to completely immerse themselves in a world, and use their imagination in a way that cannot necessarily be done when watching a feature-length film.

About James......
James' road to becoming a sequential artist started when he was in third grade and saw a Superman/Aquaman comic. He started tracing the forms, and throughout his early childhood developed a love of drawing. After high school, he rediscovered that love and attended Pratt Institute in Brooklyn NY. He remains in New York, working as a Graphic Designer for an international apparel company following his May 2011 graduation.

The Graduate

Rather go to bed supperless,
than rise in debt.

Benjamin Franklin

The Graduate

By Paul Nourigat
Illustrated by Catherine Farris

Hey sis, how was school?

All good; got a sweet grade on my math test.

Can I ask you something?

Sure.

What happened?

My friends were going on to different lives, different places, careers, more school, and so on.

You got a job, right?

Oh yeah, I decided to start bringing in the big bucks and was ready to rock my independence.

No more rules, no more pressure, just living life free and easy!

Well, what happened?

After getting the job, I had to get the car.

The car company was offering a loan with low monthly payments, so I got a new car.

Then, I bought stuff for the guy I was dating who I "thought" I was in love with.

I "had" to get the wardrobe so I was styling at work. It felt good to ditch my old school clothes.

How'd you pay for stuff, if you hadn't started your job?.

Well, that's where the story takes a BIG turn..

79

As you can see, I was barely making enough money to pay my rent and utilities, let alone groceries & my debts.

YIKES

♡ BUDGET ♡

Income

	Before	Now
Hours per month	$ 160	$ 96
Rate per hour	11.85	11.85
Total monthly earnings	**$ 1,896**	**$ 1,138**

Minus
Expenses

	Before	Now
Payroll taxes	$ (341)	$ (205)
Credit card payments	$ (340)	$ (400)
Rent share	$ (550)	$ (125)
Groceries	$ (120)	$ (120)
Clothing & personals	$ (250)	$ (50)
Cellphone & internet	$ (126)	$ (45)
Movies and fun	$ (350)	$ (25)
Car payment	$ (285)	$ (285)
Gas, insurance & service	$ (195)	$ -
Bus pass	$ -	$ (75)
Total monthly expenses	**$ (2,167)**	**$ (1,125)**

Savings

	Before	Now
Amount left over for savings	$ (271)	$ 13

plus medical, gifts, haircuts

I thought it was ok to make "minimum payments" to the credit card companies, which they will let you do.

I didn't understand that the interest expense on the money I owed would make the loan balance even larger. Each month, the debt GREW even larger.

Outstanding Balance $34,547.63

I didn't tell anyone I was in trouble until it was too late. I ignored the warning letters that kept coming.

Down deep, I was hoping they'd just go away, but instead I should have called the companies and explained my situation.

Now my credit score is in really bad shape and it will take years to get these bad marks off my credit record.

So I got evicted from my apartment and messed up my roommate's situation, because I couldn't pay my share of the rent.

Is that when the scary repo dude showed up at our house that night and took your car?

Yeah. I'm really sorry that scared you. It freaked me out too.

I didn't know they could take your stuff, even though that makes sense if you don't pay back what you owe.

Truth is, a creditor can take back just about anything and make your life pretty miserable if you don't pay what you owe.

84

From the author

A debt, such as a loan for a home or a car, may be smart ..... if it can be confidently repaid on-time.

Such decisions are highly personal and unique to each circumstance, but the theory is common to all. Don't buy what you cannot absolutely afford, given a possible loss in a job, a reduction in hours worked or at the expense of saving for your future.

Paul

If Money Could Shout ... the brutal truths for teens:

The Graduate

Illustrator Profile:
Catherine "Cat" Farris

I think credit is one of the biggest dangers that our younger generation faces, as you see in "The Graduate". It's so common these days to buy everything on credit, even small things, and we're constantly bombarded with the option to "have something now and pay for it later". It's very easy to fall into the trap of forgetting you're spending real money.

Credit can be a great tool, if it's used right. It's so important to understand how it works and how it will affect you, because used improperly, it can really ruin your life!

Why Graphic Novels?
Comics are accessible to everyone, and they're a very effective form of communication. They're the perfect combination of pictures and words that allow you to tell a story that everyone can understand.

About Cat......
Cat attended the Savannah College of Art And Design, receiving her BFA in Animation. It was her intent to eventually be a traditional-style animator for Disney, but when she graduated she says she "got sucked into comics instead!". Cat was born in Portland, OR, but also lived in Saudi Arabia, Japan, Wyoming, and Georgia. She loves baking, video games, and studying languages such as Japanese, French, and Cantonese.

The time is always right
to do what is right.

Martin Luther King, Jr.

The team gave gramps a tee-shirt that he wore to every game from then on .

From the author

Down deep, people know that others are hurting much worse than themselves, but they wait to give, thinking they will be better able to help later. Those people often never get around to helping because their needs grow and their rationale persists.

Regardless of your place in life, or your priorities or your financial strategies, you can make a positive difference in other peoples' lives. Why wait?

Paul

If Money Could Shout ... the brutal truths for teens:

Illustrator Profile:
Phil Ensberg

"Fortune Defined" was a joy to illustrate. It speaks to me on many levels and hits close to home. As a teacher, I have met families whose furniture is breaking and cars don't run, but own new flat-screen TVs and annual passes to 3 different national theme parks in Southern California. This story beautifully shows how putting "first things first" is not only the right thing to do, it can offer a more pleasurable way of life.

Why Graphic Novels?
The first comic books I owned were Tarzan #16 and #17, illustrated by John Buscema (I still have them!). I was ten when I got them, and instantly loved the comic book art form, which combines my love for art and literature. John Buscema remains one of my favorite comic book artists of all time and I enjoy reading a good graphic novel as one of life's great pleasures.

About Phil......
Phil majored in English Literature and minored in art at California Lutheran University. He now teaches Art, English, and more at The Preuss School UCSD in La Jolla, California—ranked as the #1 Transformative High School in America in 2011. In 2005, Phil was honored as the Middle School Teacher of the Year in San Diego City Schools, a job he loves and hopes to continue along with his artwork, for many years ahead.

You Call That A Job?

Things may come to those who wait,
but only the things left by those who hustle.

Abraham Lincoln

You Call That A Job?

Hey, we're hanging out tonight. You wanna come over?

Yeah, but I gotta say no.

I gotta chance for extra hours doing clean up early tomorrow morning.

By Paul Nourigat

Illustrated by Matt Merys

The regular guy is taking Saturday off so I get extra hours.

You're telling me that you'd rather sweep floors than hang with your homies?

No. Not really, ... but I've got to hit my number.

Anyway, who needs it. I've got a global net pass for the next year, rechargeable batteries, and homies all over who want to kick some tail with me. I'm a player.

You're a sweeper. You call that a job?

Rolando's room was essentially dedicated to playing video games. It had taken over his mornings, nights, and weekends.

Dude, there will be plenty of time to work after high school. This is the time of your life to accomplish something meaningful.

Let's see. You, apron burns... Me, Stratomondo level of the most sophisticated video game in history.

Hmmm .. wonder which one I'll pick?

Yeah, kiss off. I've got some big plans and I need the currency.

Truth is, it's been a different world since I stopped getting an allowance.

107

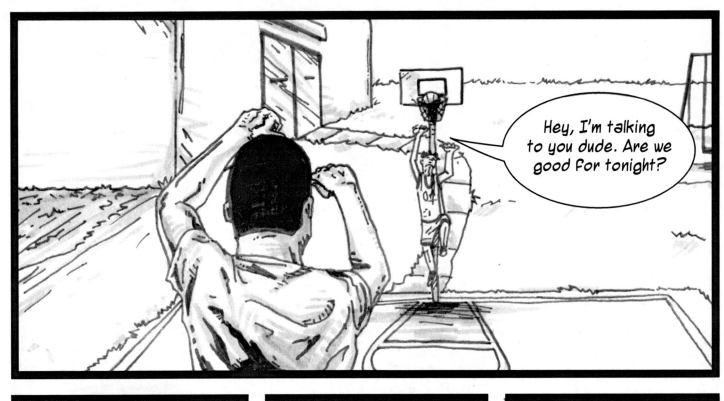

Sometimes, morning comes too soon.

When you're done out here, come inside. I want to talk to you.

The words every young employee dreads.

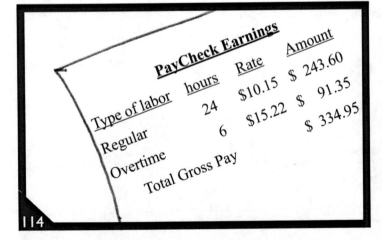

PayCheck Earnings

Type of labor	hours	Rate	Amount
Regular	24	$10.15	$ 243.60
Overtime	6	$15.22	$ 91.35
Total Gross Pay			$ 334.95

Paycheck Deductions

Federal Taxes	$ 16.75
FICA Medicare	$ 4.86
FICA OASDI	$ 14.07
State Taxes	$ 10.32
Total Deductions	$ 46.00
Net Pay	$ 288.95

115

From the author

There will always be people who want to drag you into their laziness or their bad attitudes. The best way to avoid that trap is to have a dream and pursue it.

You do not need to tell others what they should do, but instead show them through your success; success naturally occurs as you dedicate yourself to hard work and service to others.

Paul

If Money Could Shout ... the brutal truths for teens:

Illustrator Profile:
Matthew Merys

Now is an important time for everyone, particularly young people, to remember to persevere and work hard to find financial security. Having worked tons of odd jobs growing up, I remember the great feeling of getting my first "regular job" & the satisfaction of pulling in a paycheck. As a college student, it is easy for me to connect with Neilson in "You Call That A Job?"; I appreciate my paycheck!

Why Graphic Novels?
Since I was six years old I've been fascinated by comics, starting with the traditional superheroes we all know. Graphic novels build upon comics by allowing a broader range of topics. This book, "If Money Could Shout ... the brutal truths for teens", is an example of the wonderful and unique medium that opens up for artists and readers.

About Matt......
Matt is a comic book and storyboard artist who hails from Southern California, where he attends college. He's an Aries, loves his family and friends, and enjoys long walks on the beach. Majoring in Fine Arts, Matt will seek a career within the comic industry upon graduation.

THE PROMISE

Nothing in the world can take the place of persistence.
Talent will not; nothing is more common than unsuccessful men with talent.
Genius will not; unrewarded genius is almost a proverb.
Education alone will not; the world is full of educated derelicts.
Persistence and determination alone are omnipotent.

Calvin Coolidge

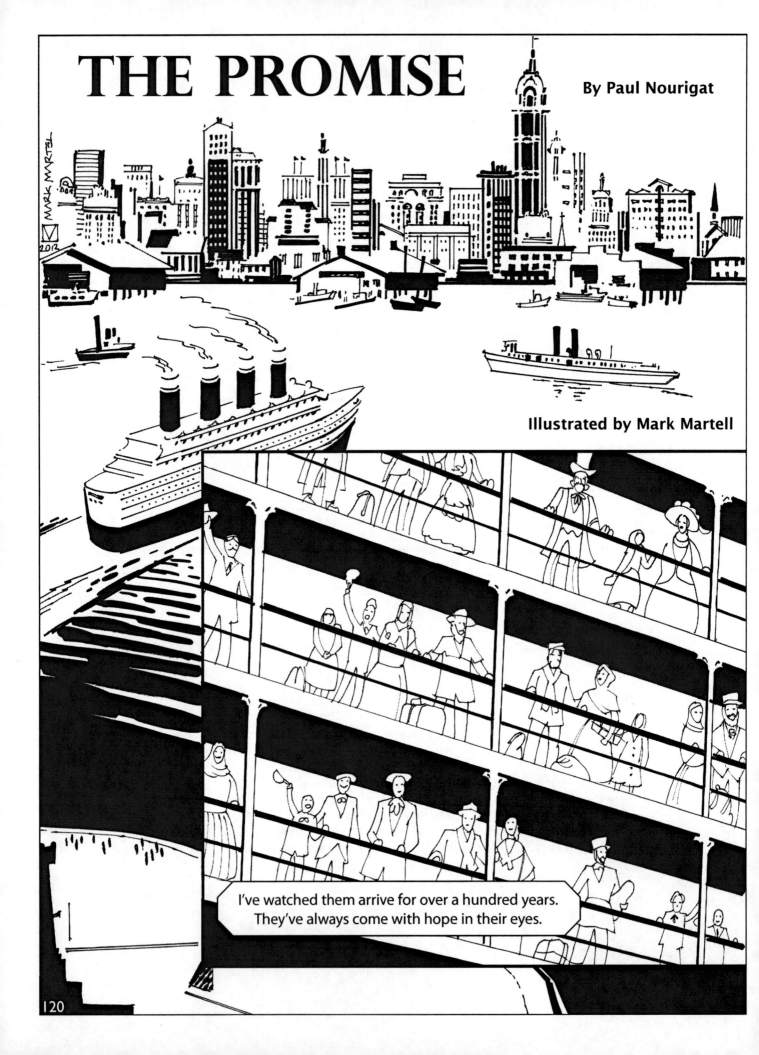

From the author

As Americans, we enjoy significantly better lives than prior generations because of the sacrifices of our parents, grandparents, and so on.

At some point, for some reason, each generation is challenged by difficult situations. In such times, certain people will toughen up, work hard, then emerge as leaders and prosper as a result.

It has always been this way.

Paul

If Money Could Shout ... the brutal truths for teens:

THE PROMISE

Illustrator Profile:
Mark Martel

Today it may seem there are no new places to go or fresh opportunities to seek out. But it has always seemed like that, until suddenly a new chance opens up. My career was like that. I felt stuck in limited art jobs I could get in the town where I live. Then an upset forced me to look online, where I found a whole new world of opportunity to do work on projects like "The Promise". Today I do art for people around the world and compete with international artists who are willing to be paid less. I've had to find those special areas where what I do is most valued.

Why Graphic Novels?
I read Steranko's "Chandler" back in the late 1970s and I fell in love with the art form. The graphic novel has evolved since then into a vibrant commercial form, flexible enough to tell all sorts of tales as well as non-fiction, like this story. I'm pleased to have been a part of the industry and a contributor to "If Money Could Shout".

About Mark......
Mark recently reconnected with his Junior High art teacher on Facebook after nearly 40 years! She had originally introduced him to many types of materials and styles, which he still uses. Mark went on to study graphic design at the Universtiy of Cincinnati for 3 years, then worked in ad agencies in Dayton, Ohio for over 25 years. Says Mark...."When I grow up, I hope to be a comic book artist!"

A final note from the author

America's strengths are grounded in our innovative and adaptive instincts. Regardless of what's thrown at us, we figure it out and we do what's needed to move forward.

Each teen has to ask themself whether they want to be in control of their financial future, or dependent on the leftovers of others. For me, there was nothing more exciting than learning I could stand on my own, by working hard and practicing the disciplines shown in these stories.

"Life" is tough enough. Once you decide to be financially intelligent, you'll find that "life" gets much easier.

Paul

About the Author

Over a twenty-eight year consulting career, Paul Nourigat has advised families, businesses, and community leaders across the country.

In addition to his time spent with thousands of highly successful people, he has invested extensive time with families who are struggling with money. As a result, Paul developed a clear understanding of "what works" and "what doesn't" in business and personal finance.

Having heard over and over "I wish I had learned more about money when I was young", Paul set out on a mission to teach young people about money using a very unique approach. "If Money Could Shout" is Paul's 7th financial literacy book, following the five book series "Marvels of Money for kids" and "Why is there Money" oriented to K-5.

Blending extensive graphics and fictional stories which young people connect with, Paul is breaking new ground by using the graphic novel format to teach financial literacy to teens.

Discover Paul's financial tips and tools at
www.MarvelsOfMoney.org

Other books from the author:

"Marvels of Money ... for kids" (5-book series for ages 7-11 years)
Richly illustrated, engaging and practical stories for young readers about the fundamentals of money.

Earning Excitement ..... Kids want things that they don't have. When should they stop asking for things and earn them instead? Earning Excitement tells a story about Jack and Chelsea's patience, self-sufficiency, and the steps kids can take to earn something.

Spending Success ...... There are so many things kids want to buy! But they cannot afford them all. Spending Success tells a story about Chelsea and Jack's great success with financial priority setting, against a backdrop of peer pressure and media influence.

Debt Dangers .... Borrowing money sounds easy, given the advertisements kids hear. Debt Dangers shows how Chelsea and Jack make decisions about borrowing, when loans may be appropriate, and why it is best for kids to say no and live within their means.

Giving Greatness .... There is great need all around us. How can kids help? Giving Greatness is a touching and timely story, as Chelsea and Jack show how they, their families and their friends can help those in need.

Terrific Tools ... for money ...... Which tools should a kid use to manage money? Terrific Tools is a story about Chelsea and Jack learning how financial tools are used in different settings and the importance of privacy and security of information.

Why is there Money? (For younger readers, ages 5-8 years)
This poetic journey through history shows the path from bartering to currencies, to credit, to the modern financial tools used by adults. Kids will enjoy the beautiful images as they visualize the fascinating evolution of world commerce.

Tools and resources can be found at
www.MarvelsOfMoney.org

7/28/15

CPSIA information can be obtained at www.ICGtesting.com
Printed in the USA
LVOW09s1929010715

444612LV00012B/524/P

9 781477 488041